M000025042

Forever Grateful To You:

Made in United States
North Haven, CT
13 December 2022

28722946R00065